# LIVING IN THE WILD: PRIMATES

GORILLAS

Lori McManus

**www.raintreepublishers.co.uk**

Visit our website to find out more information about Raintree books.

**To order:**

☎ Phone 0845 6044371
▤ Fax +44 (0) 1865 312263
🖳 Email myorders@raintreepublishers.co.uk

Customers from outside the UK please telephone +44 1865 312262

Raintree is an imprint of Capstone Global Library Limited, a company incorporated in England and Wales having its registered office at 7 Pilgrim Street, London, EC4V 6LB – Registered company number: 6695582

Edited by Abby Colich, Jilly Hunt, and Vaarunika Dharmapala
Designed by Victoria Allen
Picture research by Tracy Cummins
Original illustrations © Capstone Global Library Ltd 2012
Illustrations by Oxford Designers & Illustrators and HL Studios
Originated by Capstone Global Library Ltd
Printed and bound in China by CTPS

ISBN 978 1 406 23303 2 (hardback)
16 15 14 13 12
10 9 8 7 6 5 4 3 2 1

ISBN 978 1 406 23310 0 (paperback)
17 16 15 14 13
10 9 8 7 6 5 4 3 2 1

**British Library Cataloguing in Publication Data**
McManus, Lori.
Gorillas. -- (Living in the wild. Primates)
599.8'83-dc22
A full catalogue record for this book is available from the British Library.

**Acknowledgements**
We would like to thank the following for permission to reproduce photographs: Alamy p. 41 (© Orokiet); Corbis pp. 15 (© Yann Arthus-Bertrand), 35 (© Bettmann); FLPA pp. 8 (Terry Whittaker), 17 (Ariadne Van Zandbergen), 26 (Terry Whittaker), 27 (Konrad Wothe/Minden Pictures), 34 (Konrad Wothe); Getty Images pp. 25 (Buena Vista Images), 28 (Andy Rouse); istockphoto pp. 7 (© Elliot Hurwitt), 20 (© DaveThomasNZ), 44 (© Elliot Hurwitt); National Geographic Stock pp. 6 (Joel Sartore), 13 (Michael Nichols), 23 (Suzi Eszterhas/Minden Pictures), 24 (Peter G. Veit), 29 (Ian Nichols), 36 (Gerry Ellis/Minden Pictures), 39 (Michael Nichols); Newscom p. 33 (CB2/ZOB/WENN.com); Photolibrary pp. 4 (Berndt Fischer), 37 (Michel Gunther); Photoshot p. 19 (Andy Rouse/NHPA); Shutterstock pp. 9 (© Alan Jeffery) 11 (© Ronald van der Beek), 24 (© Steffen Foerster Photography), 22 (© Eric Gevaert), 31 (© Peter J. Kovacs), 32 (© neelsky), 43 (© Eric Gevaert).

Cover photograph of a mountain gorilla in Rwanda, reproduced with permission of Photolibrary (J-L. Klein & M-L. Hubert).

Every effort has been made to contact copyright holders of any material reproduced in this book. Any omissions will be rectified in subsequent printings if notice is given to the publisher.

# Contents

Some words are shown in bold, **like this**. You can find out what they mean by looking in the glossary.

# What are primates?

Out of the bushes roll a group of youngsters playing follow the leader. Several adults relax near by. Is this a playground at a park? No, it is a forest in Africa where young gorillas play while their mothers watch.

## Six key characteristics

Gorillas belong to a special group of animals called primates. Monkeys, lemurs, orangutans, and humans belong to this group. Primates are **mammals** that share six key characteristics:

1. Forward-facing eyes – both eyes point in the same direction and can focus on the same object.

2. Eye sockets – the eyeball sits inside a hollow space protected by bone.

3. Grasping hands – the thumb can be used to grip or press against the other four fingers.

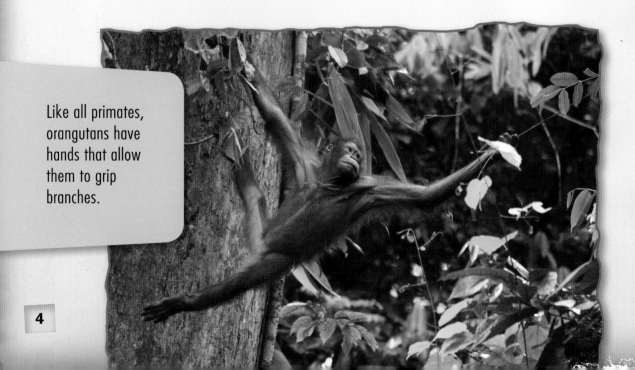

Like all primates, orangutans have hands that allow them to grip branches.

**4.** Nails – most primates have fingers and toes ending in a flat nail that protects the tip.

**5.** Fingerprints – the skin on the fingertips and underside of the hand is bare and covered in a pattern of tiny ridges. Each primate's fingerprints are unique.

**6.** Large brains relative to their body size – compared to many mammals, primates have large brains which give them higher intelligence.

All primates, except for humans, are currently **endangered**. These special animals may soon disappear completely if they are not protected.

This map shows where in the world non-human primates live.

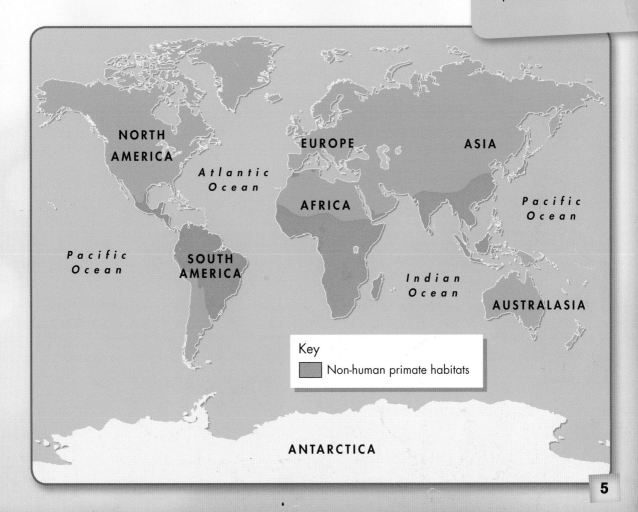

# What are gorillas?

Gorillas are the largest and heaviest primate. They are part of a group called apes, which also includes chimpanzees, orangutans, bonobos, gibbons, and humans. All apes have a large body size and weight. They have broad chests and long arms. Apes have big brains, and do not have tails. Gorillas share similarities with other apes, yet their specific size, shape, and colour set them apart.

Like all apes, this gorilla does not have a tail outside its body.

## Size and shape

Gorillas are the largest apes on Earth. Males are always bigger than females. When standing upright, gorillas are about 13 centimetres (5 inches) shorter than average human adults. Although some male gorillas grow as heavy as 250 kilograms (550 pounds), most males weigh between 135 and 200 kilograms (300 and 440 pounds). Females weigh about 70–90 kilograms (150–200 pounds).

A gorilla's shape is unusual among non-human apes. Its stomach is larger than its chest! This huge belly is due to the size of a gorilla's intestines, the stretchy tube attached to the stomach that absorbs **nutrients** from food. A gorilla's small intestine would be nearly 10 metres (33 feet) long if it were stretched out straight!

Gorillas' arms are much longer than their legs. They also have bigger muscles in their arms. Gorillas use their powerful arms for walking and finding food. They almost always walk on their hands and feet, even though they can stand up on their legs.

A gorilla's belly is even larger than its wide, powerful chest.

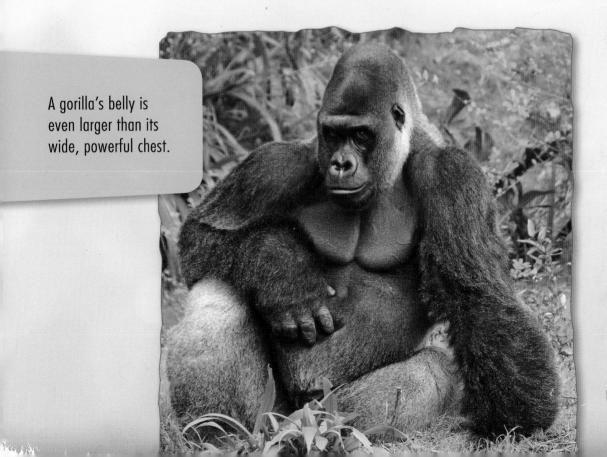

## Hair and skin

Gorillas have dark black to brown-grey hair. This hair can be long and silky or short and thin, depending on where the gorillas live. As male gorillas age, the hair on their backs and upper thighs turns silvery grey. Because of this change in colour, adult males are sometimes called "silverbacks".

Under a gorilla's dark hair, the skin is also dark. Sometimes baby gorillas are born with patches of lighter skin that turn dark with age. Gorillas have skin without hair on the soles of their feet, palms of their hands, fingers, nose, lips, ears, and chest.

Gorillas have especially tough skin on their fingers. They use their knuckles for walking, and the thick skin protects them from injury. Gorillas, chimpanzees, and bonobos are the only animals to get around by "knuckle-walking".

Gorillas can move very fast when they knuckle-walk.

## A big head

Gorillas have large heads. The back part of the head is higher than the front. This bony area, called the sagittal crest, supports the strong muscles needed to chew raw plants. A gorilla's large forehead protects its small eyes.

Another obvious feature on a gorilla's face is its wide, flat nose. Its nostrils are large. Although gorillas have a good sense of smell, they rely more on their eyesight than their sense of smell.

### NOSEPRINTS

Scientists can tell gorillas apart by looking at their noses. Each gorilla's nose is unique, like a fingerprint.

Here you can see a gorilla's wide, flat nose, its large forehead, and the sagittal crest on the back of the head.

# How are gorillas classified?

Scientists **classify** gorillas into two main groups based on their similarities.

## Classification of living things

All animals share basic characteristics. For example, they all eat food to get energy. However, some animals are more closely related than others.

Scientists usually divide living things into seven levels of classification: kingdom, phylum, class, order, family, genus, and **species**. These can be divided even further, for example, into suborder and family.

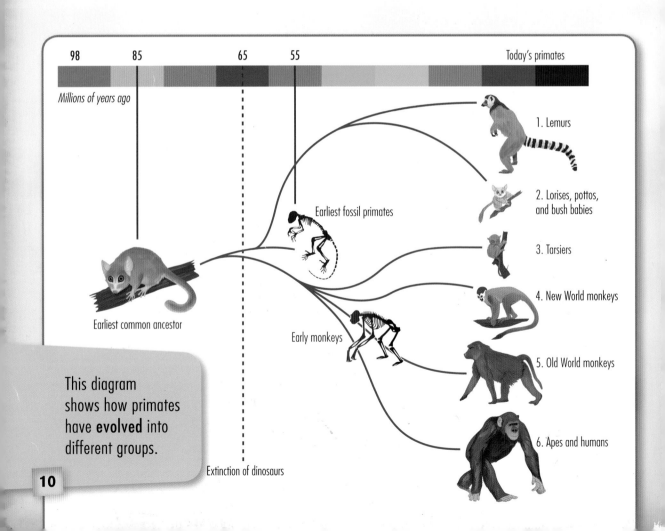

98    85          65        55                              Today's primates

*Millions of years ago*

Earliest fossil primates

Earliest common ancestor

Early monkeys

1. Lemurs

2. Lorises, pottos, and bush babies

3. Tarsiers

4. New World monkeys

5. Old World monkeys

6. Apes and humans

This diagram shows how primates have **evolved** into different groups.

Extinction of dinosaurs

# Classification of gorillas

Scientists once believed that all gorillas were similar enough to be classified as one species. However, gorillas in western Africa are smaller and have shorter hair than other gorillas. Eastern gorillas grow larger and have darker hair. In 2001, scientists classified gorillas into two species: the western gorilla and the eastern gorilla. These two species can be divided into even smaller groups, called subspecies – western lowland gorilla, (western) Cross River gorilla, eastern lowland gorilla, and (eastern) mountain gorilla.

Kingdom: Animalia

Phylum: Chordata

Subphylum: Vertebrata

Class: Mammalia

Order: Primates

Suborder: Haplorrhini

Family: Hominidae

Genus: Gorilla

Species: Gorilla gorilla

This diagram shows how the western lowland gorilla (below) is classified.

# Where do gorillas live?

Gorillas live in **tropical** and **sub-tropical** forests in Africa. Some of the forests are in the mountains, and some cover areas of low, wet land. Gorillas live in these **habitats** because of the plants, trees, and rain.

AFRICA

N

INDIAN OCEAN

Key

Western lowland gorillas

Eastern lowland gorillas

Mountain gorillas

0      1000 miles

0      1000 kilometres

This map shows where three of the four gorilla subspecies live. However, there are so few Cross River gorillas left that they cannot be shown here.

## Forest habitats

Gorillas do well in tropical and sub-tropical forest habitats. A tropical forest is a forest of tall trees that grows where the temperature is warm all year. Sub-tropical forests also have tall trees, but they are a little further from the equator and not quite as warm. Because of the higher **elevation** in their habitat, mountain gorillas experience cooler temperatures than other gorilla subspecies, especially at night.

The amount of rain determines the kinds of plants that grow in forest habitats. Some forests get a lot of rain, more than 250 centimetres (100 inches) a year. These forests are called **rainforests**. Gorillas who live in rainforests benefit from the many leafy plants that grow where water is plentiful.

## Lowland gorillas

Some gorillas live in tropical forests that grow where the land is flat and low. The gorillas in these areas are called lowland gorillas. Lowland areas usually have a rainy season and a dry season. Plants in lowland areas include succulents (plants that can store water inside their cells) and thorny, short bushes. These plants provide lowland gorillas with food.

Lowland tropical forests sometimes have natural clearings where grasses and water plants grow. These are good food for lowland gorillas.

## Mountain gorillas

Mountain gorillas live in the Virunga Mountain Range in Uganda, Rwanda, and the Democratic Republic of Congo. During the rainy season, mountain gorillas live among tall trees with smooth bark and thick bushes. They eat the bark, leaves, stems, and fruits of these plants. During drier months, mountain gorillas move to areas where they can eat bamboo.

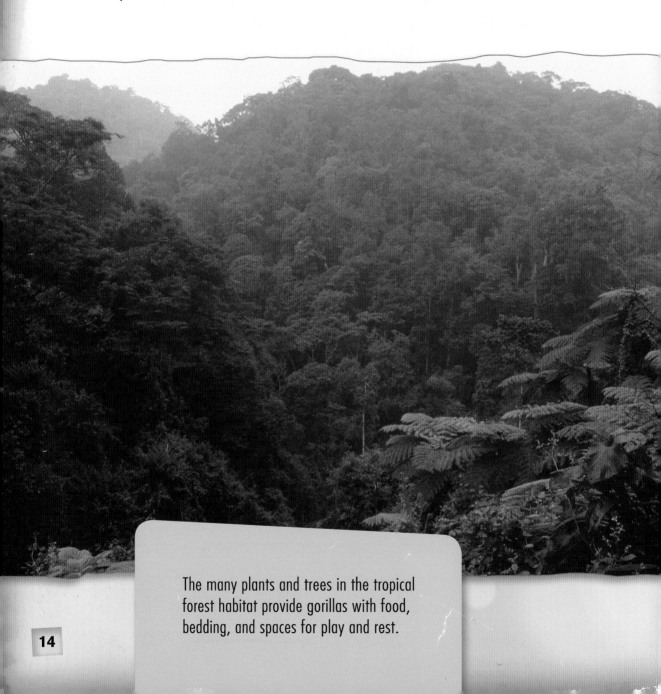

The many plants and trees in the tropical forest habitat provide gorillas with food, bedding, and spaces for play and rest.

## DIAN FOSSEY

In 1966, Dian Fossey began studying mountain gorillas in eastern Africa. At first, the gorillas ran away whenever she tried to approach. Then she began to quietly copy the gorillas' behaviour. She climbed trees and chomped on wild celery. Soon, Fossey could sit close to the gorillas without scaring them. She took photographs of the gorillas and studied their behaviour for almost 20 years.

Dian Fossey worked hard to protect the mountain gorillas. She tried to stop hunters and people who wanted to make money by showing the gorillas to visitors. She also tried to keep cows from eating the grasses in the gorillas' habitat. Her work made poachers (illegal hunters) and farmers angry. Fossey was killed in Rwanda in 1985, probably by people who wanted to stop her work.

An organization that Dian Fossey started in 1978 still exists. It is called the Dian Fossey Gorilla Fund International and still works to help protect gorillas.

Dian Fossey became the first human to experience a friendly touch by a mountain gorilla.

# What adaptations help gorillas survive?

Over time, gorillas have developed characteristics that help them survive in the forests of Africa. These characteristics and behaviours are called **adaptations**. Mountain gorillas possess slightly different adaptations from lowland gorillas.

## Arms and legs

A gorilla's long arms and short legs make it easy for it to walk on all fours. This way of walking spreads out the gorilla's heavy weight on to both its arms and legs. If a gorilla had to walk on just its legs, its bones, knees, and hips would soon wear down from the weight.

### TUG-OF-WAR

Scientists estimate that a gorilla is over six times stronger than a human. A gorilla would win a game of tug-of-war even if six adult men were pulling on the other side!

Because gorillas are so large, they are not as fast or as flexible as other primates. They are not able to swing easily from tree branch to tree branch. Instead, gorillas use their long, strong arms to pull down branches, rip thick plants from the ground, and climb trees to find food.

# Hands and feet

Gorillas have **opposable thumbs** and opposable big toes. This means that the thumb and big toe can face and touch the other fingers and toes. This allows gorillas to grasp small objects such as insects and vines with their hands and feet. The gorillas' grip also allows them to hold their babies carefully, peel stems, and build nests for sleeping.

Here you can see a gorilla's opposable big toe.

## Look out for those teeth!

Gorillas have 32 teeth, many of which are huge molars. These molars allow gorillas to grind up tough plant parts so they can be swallowed. Gorillas also have teeth called canines. These pointy teeth are found on the sides of the mouth and help with ripping.

Male gorillas' canines are especially big. The males use these large, sharp teeth to defend females and their young from predators (animals that eat other animals) such as leopards.

## Keeping warm

Gorillas must keep warm to survive. This is not a problem for lowland gorillas, as the temperatures where they live rarely drop below 20°C (68°F). However, some mountain gorillas live high up enough to experience near freezing temperatures at night.

Mountain gorillas have developed long, thick hair to keep them warm. In contrast, lowland gorillas have short hair. The hair on all gorillas protects them from insect bites.

Gorillas have also developed behaviours to keep themselves warm. On cold days, gorillas huddle close together for long periods of time. They use each other's body heat to stay warm.

### BODY ODOUR!

Gorillas sweat! The sweat helps protect their skin from dry cracks. Male gorillas also produce a strong sweat odour when they are stressed or excited. The smell helps the males to communicate their emotions to other gorillas.

These mountain gorillas have long,
thick hair to keep them warm.

# What do gorillas eat?

Gorillas are herbivores, which means they mainly eat plants. Gorillas are not known to kill other animals for food and few animals attack or feed on gorillas.

The types of plants gorillas eat depend on where they live. Mountain gorillas usually eat green plant parts such as leaves, vines, and stems. They also eat small amounts of fruit, roots, and tiny creatures such as worms and snails. Eastern lowland gorillas eat plants, and fruits when they can find them. Western lowland gorillas eat a lot of fruit as well as leaves, stems, and seeds.

Gorillas will travel outside their normal living area to find special food such as young bamboo stems.

# A giant appetite

Gorillas spend about a third of their day eating. An adult male will eat up to 20 kilograms (45 pounds) of food each day. That is about the weight of a six-year-old child! Gorillas eat so much in order to get all the **nutrients** their large bodies need.

Gorillas are picky about their food. They will peel off the stem of a plant to eat the soft part inside. They leave behind the parts of the plants they do not like. Gorillas rarely drink water. Instead, the plants they eat contain the water they need. Gorillas also suck rainwater from their hair.

# Top of the chain

A food chain is made up of a series of living things that are each dependent on the next as a source of food. Gorillas are usually at the top of their food chain.

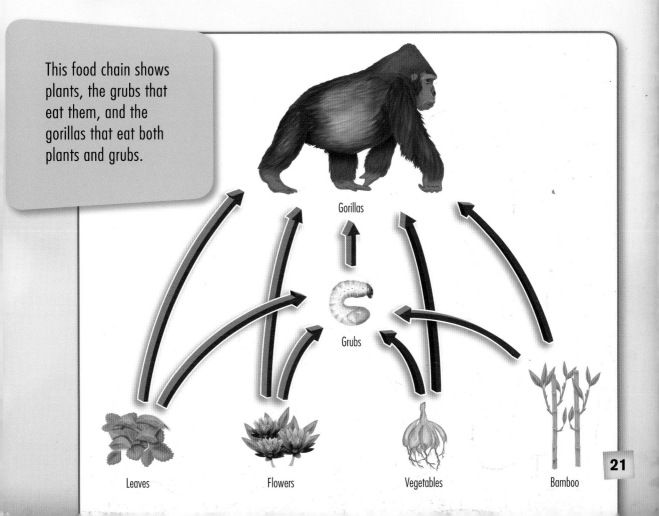

This food chain shows plants, the grubs that eat them, and the gorillas that eat both plants and grubs.

Gorillas

Grubs

Leaves          Flowers          Vegetables          Bamboo

# What is a gorilla's life cycle?

Gorillas experience different stages of life, just as humans do. Gorillas are babies first, then children, and finally adults. When they are adults, gorillas can produce babies. The stages of growth from a creature's birth to its death are called its life cycle.

## A baby is born

A baby gorilla grows inside its mother's body for about 8½ months. At birth, the baby gorilla weighs about 2 kilograms (4½ pounds). The baby starts drinking its mother's milk immediately. It depends on its mother for food, warmth, and protection.

Baby gorillas learn to climb on to their mothers' backs when they are six to seven months old. They hold on tight while their mother moves around.

Baby gorillas grow quickly. They begin to crawl at about nine weeks old. At about six to seven months old, baby gorillas can walk short distances. They start to eat plants, but also keep drinking their mother's milk until they are about two years old.

Play is very important for young gorillas. They chase, wrestle, and join in games with each other. Baby gorillas also play with adults, jumping on them and giving them gentle bites.

## Juvenile gorillas

Between the ages of three and six, young gorillas are known as juveniles. Juveniles practise skills such as peeling stems by copying the older gorillas. A juvenile gorilla still stays close to its mother, sharing her nest until she has her next baby three or four years later.

Juvenile gorillas like climbing trees. Since they are smaller and lighter than adults, they can climb more easily to find leaves high above the ground.

# Teenage gorillas

Gorillas move into a stage called adolescence when they are about six years old. During this stage, they begin to turn into adults. They gain weight and grow larger. They become skilled at finding food. During adolescence, males grow taller and start to look different from females. The adolescent males are called "blackbacks" because, unlike the adult males, the hair on their backs is dark.

Here you can see adolescent males, a female, a baby, and an adult male. Can you tell which is which?

## Adulthood

Gorillas reach adulthood when they are able to reproduce (have babies of their own). A female reaches adulthood at about eight years old. Most females have their first babies by the age of ten. Female gorillas usually have one baby at a time, every three to four years.

Male gorillas are fully grown and able to reproduce at about 11 or 12 years of age. At this time, silvery grey hair grows across their backs and they become "silverbacks". Often, the new adult is chased away by the male leader of his group. The young silverback then starts a group of his own or takes over another silverback's group. As the leader of a group, the silverback will mate with the group's two or three female gorillas.

Gorillas live to about 35 years of age in the wild. In zoos, they can live up to the age of 50. Gorillas lose their teeth as they grow older. Without teeth, eating is difficult. An old gorilla becomes thin and weak.

This female gorilla is pregnant.

# How do gorillas behave?

Gorillas live together in family groups. The gorillas within a group eat, relax, and sleep close to one another.

## Living in troops

A gorilla family group is called a troop. Each troop usually has 5 to 10 members, but some have up to 30. One strong male silverback leads the troop. Other members include one or two adolescent males, two or three females, and several juveniles and babies.

As the leader of the troop, the silverback makes all the decisions. The silverback decides where the troop will travel, when they will eat, and when they will rest. The silverback mates with each of the females in the troop. He is the father of all the young gorillas. Although gorillas are usually peaceful, a silverback will fight to protect his troop from predators such as crocodiles and humans.

Each troop is led by a silverback male.

# Home range

The gorilla troop lives and travels in one general area. This area is called a home range. A troop's home range covers 2.5 to 16 square kilometres (1 to 6 square miles). Since many different kinds of plants grow in **tropical** forests, gorillas usually do not have to travel far to find food. Yet a troop always moves to a new eating space each day. This behaviour saves forest plants from being destroyed.

Sometimes the home range of one troop overlaps with the home range of another. Gorillas usually do not fight over their area. Instead, the silverback leader simply moves his troop a safe distance away.

Troop members spread out when they eat to avoid arguments over food.

## How do new troops form?

Once a young silverback becomes an adult, he sets out to form his own troop. Sometimes he attracts females from other troops to join him. Or he might try to take over a troop from an older silverback by scaring him away. Silverbacks might even fight for the leadership of a troop. If the younger silverback loses, he will often spend time with other young adult males before he tries to win his own troop again.

Silverbacks try to scare their enemies away by showing their teeth, roaring, and beating their chests.

When a female gorilla becomes an adult, she leaves her family troop to join a new one. The female must respect the silverback in the new group. If the silverback does not earn her trust, the female may leave. Some females change troops two or three times before they settle down.

In a troop, a female's importance depends on how long she has known the silverback. Often, a female gorilla tries to join a silverback who is alone. That way, she automatically becomes the most important female in the troop.

## Who grooms whom?

Gorillas groom each other based on their relationships. Grooming is when one animal cleans another animal's hair and skin. Younger females in a troop argue over who gets to groom the silverback. They want to win his approval. Usually, females do not groom each other but every mother carefully grooms her young.

It is their mother's responsibility to groom these young gorillas. At the moment, they are busy playing!

# A DAY IN THE LIFE OF A GORILLA

Gorillas spend most of their time eating and resting. They get up early in the morning when the sun rises. The troop moves to the spot where they will feed for the day. Then the gorillas eat all morning.

With full bellies, gorillas relax for four to six hours in the middle of the day. The babies and juveniles play with each other. The adults rest as they watch the young ones. Gorillas also use this rest time to cuddle. In the late afternoon, they set out to eat for a few more hours. Then they settle in for a long night's sleep when the sun goes down.

## READY FOR BED

Gorillas make new sleeping nests every night. They gather leaves, twigs, and branches to tuck under and around themselves. Each gorilla makes its own nest, except for young ones under three years old. The babies sleep with their mothers.

## LOOKING FOR MIZA

In 2007, a baby gorilla called Miza and her mother disappeared from their family group in Virunga National Park. Miza's father, a silverback named Kabirizi, immediately moved his family group to a hiding spot high in the mountains. Then he searched for Miza and her mother. After several days, Kabirizi found Miza in the forest. Sadly, Miza's mother was never found. Miza's story has been recorded in a book called *Looking for Miza*.

This western lowland gorilla is eating a meal of leaves.

# How intelligent are gorillas?

Gorillas have large heads that contain large brains. These big, complex brains make them capable of learning, remembering, using tools, and communicating with each other. Gorillas are curious animals.

Young gorillas learn skills by copying older gorillas and then practising. For example, baby gorillas try to make their own sleeping nests from the time they are 18 months old. At first, the young gorillas only pull a few grass stems over themselves. With practice over the next two years, they learn how to make tidy, comfortable nests.

Baby gorillas learn new skills by copying the behaviour of older gorillas.

## Using tools

In 2005, scientists observed gorillas using tools for the first time. A female gorilla in the Democratic Republic of Congo used a stick to test the depth of water before wading into a river. A second gorilla used a tree stump as a bridge. Since 2005, scientists have observed other wild gorillas using rocks to smash open palm nuts. In Cameroon, Cross River gorillas have used sticks, rocks, and dirt clods to chase away humans.

### SET FREE

Damian Aspinall raised a baby gorilla called Kwibi at his **conservation** organization in Kent. When Kwibi was five years old, Aspinall released him into a **rainforest** in West Africa. Five years later in 2010, Aspinall returned to the spot of Kwibi's release. He called for Kwibi using sounds from the gorilla's childhood. Amazingly, Kwibi recognized the sounds and Aspinall. Kwibi immediately sat down next to Aspinall. Then he playfully climbed on Aspinall's back.

Damian Aspinall is reunited with Kwibi as several members of Kwibi's troop look on.

# Gorilla communication

Gorillas make 22 different sounds to express love, joy, fear, sadness, anger, pride, and other emotions. When gorillas are happy, they make purring sounds. When they are upset, they cough or bark. A low rumbling sound can be heard when gorillas are laughing. Gorillas even cry, using soft sounds rather than tears. Baby gorillas whimper or scream if they are scared or left alone.

Gorillas also communicate emotions with the expressions on their faces. With a stern look, the lead silverback can stop his females from arguing. When angry, gorillas press their lips firmly together and stare straight ahead. When afraid, gorillas open their mouths wide, show their teeth, and shift their eyes back and forth. Young gorillas smile when they are play-fighting.

Gorillas use body movements to communicate. This male is beating his chest to scare off an enemy. The "pok-pok" noise of the chest beating can be heard over 200 metres (650 feet) away!

# FRANCINE "PENNY" PATTERSON

Francine "Penny" Patterson has studied communication between gorillas and humans for almost 40 years. In 1972, she began working with a one-year-old gorilla named Koko. Over time, Patterson taught Koko over 1,000 words in sign language. Patterson says that Koko also understands about 2,000 English words. Koko responds with sign language or obedience to a command.

Patterson established the Gorilla Foundation with other scientists. This organization works to protect wild gorillas and study gorilla intelligence.

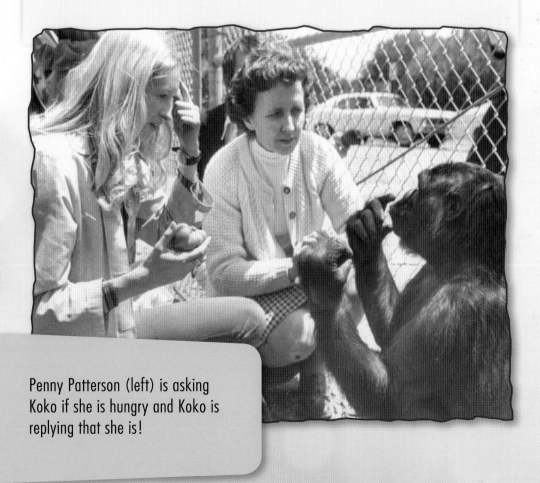

Penny Patterson (left) is asking Koko if she is hungry and Koko is replying that she is!

# What threats do gorillas face?

Gorillas are **endangered** animals. They may become **extinct** because of hunting, loss of their **habitat**, and disease. Humans are the greatest threat to gorillas.

## Hunting gorillas

Gorillas are often hunted for their meat. Many people in Africa are poor and need food. They cannot afford to buy expensive meats such as pork or chicken. So they buy the meat of wild animals such as gorillas and elephants. Meat from wild animals is called bushmeat. Hunters make money by selling bushmeat to restaurants and local people. Hunters often break the law by killing gorillas on protected land.

Some people hunt gorillas for sport. They want to collect parts of gorillas to show off to others. Sadly, a gorilla's hands or head may be turned into a trophy. Sometimes, hunters set traps for other animals, and gorillas accidentally get caught in them.

If a gorilla gets caught in a trap like this, it can be seriously injured or even die.

# Habitat loss

As human populations grow, people look for new places to live and work. Sometimes people cut down the trees in African forests to make space for farms and houses. People also use the trees for firewood.

Companies clear trees off the land to make money. Mining companies want to dig for a metal called coltan. Coltan is used to make mobile phones. Other companies chop down the trees so that the wood can be used to build houses.

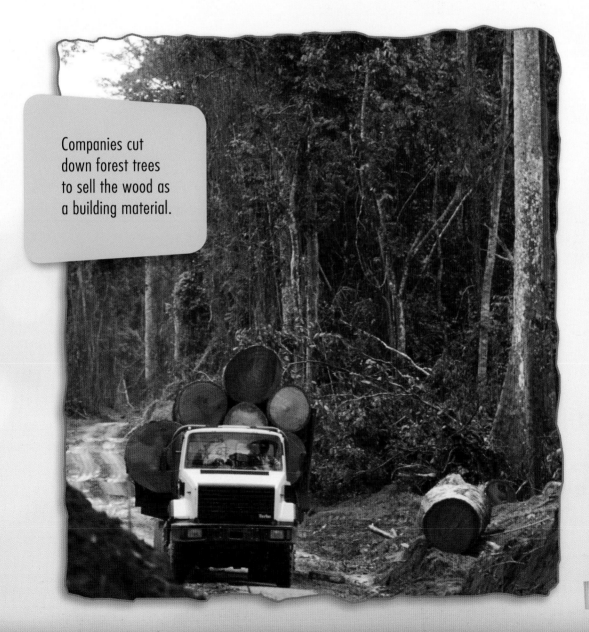

Companies cut down forest trees to sell the wood as a building material.

## Problems for gorillas

As people cut down the forests, gorillas must move to new places or live in open areas. Mountain gorillas have begun to live higher up in the mountains, but the cold, wet temperatures at these heights can cause illness. Cleared land makes food hard to find for lowland gorillas.

With the trees and bushes gone, some gorillas search for food in farmers' fields. Often, people attack the gorillas to scare them away. The silverback leader will try to defend his troop. He may be killed and the troop will scatter. The gorillas are unlikely to survive without their leader.

### EASY PICKINGS

Cleared land makes hunting gorillas easier. **Tropical** forests are often too thick with trees for humans to move quickly. With cleared land, hunters can use vehicles to get close to the gorillas.

## Diseases

Safari holidays to see the gorillas in Africa are popular. Money paid by the visitors helps the local people. However, people can spread diseases to gorillas if they get too close. Gorillas do not have any protection from many human diseases. A disease such as measles can be deadly.

## Why should humans care about gorillas?

Gorillas are quiet, peaceful animals that present no danger to humans unless they are threatened. They help keep the forest habitat healthy. Gorillas eat and distribute seeds so new plants will grow. If gorillas become extinct, the chance to know more about these "gentle giants" would be lost forever.

It can be thrilling to see gorillas up close in the wild. However, if the gorillas become too comfortable around humans, they may be less likely to run away from hunters.

# How can people help gorillas?

Humans are the main reason that gorillas are **endangered**. However, humans are also working hard to save gorillas and **conserve** their **habitats**.

## Conservation organizations

**Conservation** organizations raise money to rescue and nurse injured gorillas. They also help enforce laws against poaching and help poor people find food sources other than bushmeat. Some conservation groups work to protect gorilla habitats from being destroyed.

## What can you do?

- You can join conservation groups, such as the World Wildlife Fund (WWF) and Conservation International, and perhaps donate some pocket money every now and then.

- Encourage your family not to buy furniture made from the wood of **rainforest** trees.

- If you go shopping for food with your parents, you can ask them to buy goods that have been produced in an environmentally friendly way. Food labels will give information on this. Fairtrade goods ensure that money is earned by local people, which may mean they do not have to take part in activities that may harm gorillas.

- Read about gorillas and tell your friends and family about what you find out. The more people who know about endangered gorillas, the better.

- Finally, make sure you recycle as much as possible. This means that materials such as wood can be saved and reused rather than more trees being cut down.

Scientists believe there may be only about 200 Cross River gorillas left. The Cross River gorilla is the most endangered of all gorilla subspecies.

# What does the future hold for gorillas?

The future of gorillas is not certain. These gentle giants will face extinction if their **habitats** disappear and if they continue to be hunted in large numbers.

However, there is hope for gorillas. **Conservation** organizations have helped to keep the numbers of living gorillas more constant. African governments are working to maintain peace so people will travel to see the gorillas. With holidays called "eco-tours", local people earn money by leading groups through the forest in ways that are safe for the animals and the visitors. Individuals and groups around the world are working hard to save the gorillas and their forest habitats.

## WALKING TALL

The Aspinall Foundation rescues ill or injured gorillas. One of the foundation's rescued gorillas, Ambam, has become quite famous. In 2010, an animal researcher filmed the 21-year-old silverback strolling around on just his feet. The researcher posted the video on YouTube. Thousands of people have now watched Ambam walk around like a human. Scientists believe Ambam walks upright rather than on all fours so that he can carry food with his hands and see over the wall at feeding time.

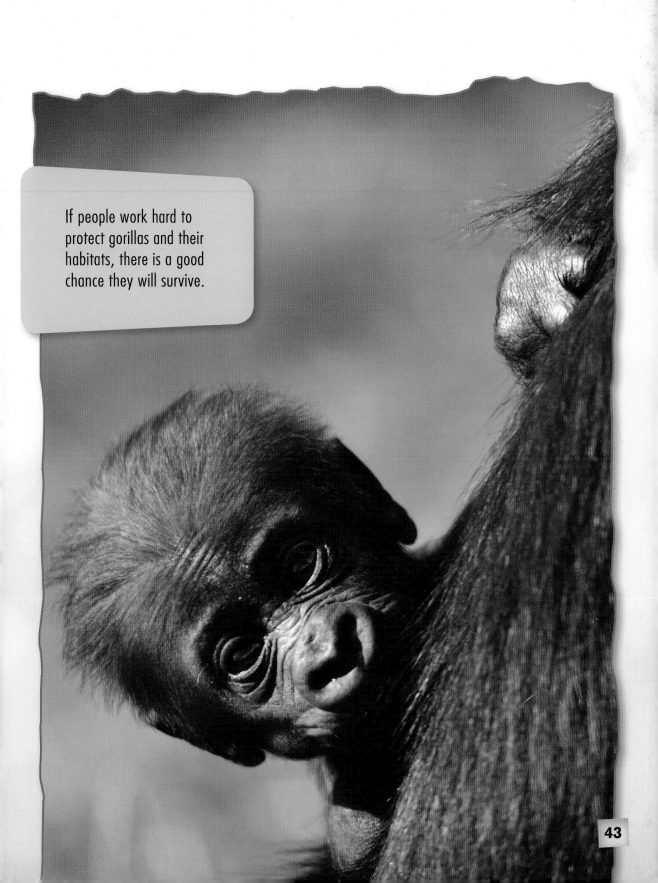

If people work hard to protect gorillas and their habitats, there is a good chance they will survive.

# Gorilla profile

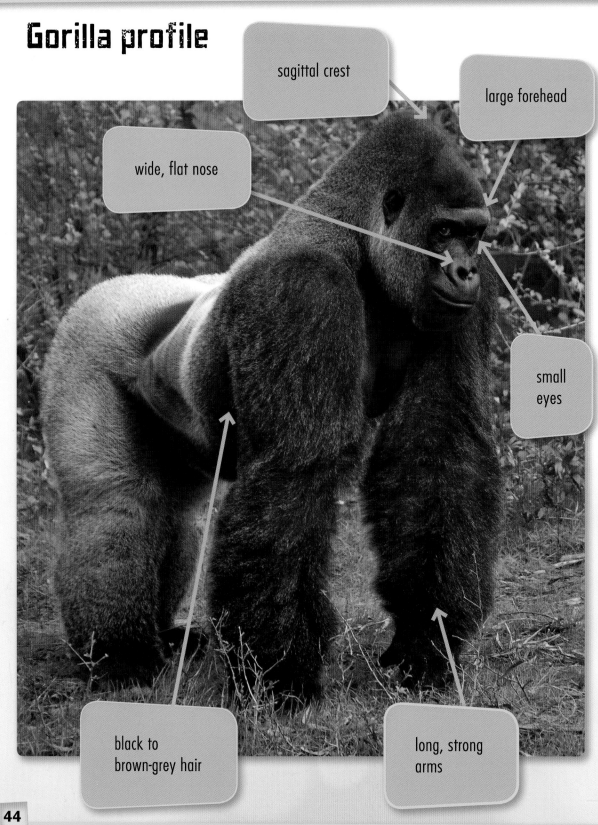

sagittal crest

large forehead

wide, flat nose

small eyes

black to brown-grey hair

long, strong arms

**Species:** western gorilla

**Weight:** adult males 135 to 220 kilograms (300 to 500 pounds); adult females 70 to 90 kilograms (150 to 200 pounds)

**Height:** adult males 1.7 to 1.8 metres (5 feet 7 inches to 6 feet); adult females up to 1.5 metres (5 feet)

**Habitat: tropical** mountain and lowland forests

**Diet:** fruit, leaves, stems, flowers, seeds, bark, roots, and some insects

**Number of young:** a single infant after 8½ months of pregnancy. Females will give birth about every 4 years after they have reached maturity at about 8 years of age.

**Birth weight:** 1.8–2.3 kilograms (4–5 pounds)

**Life expectancy:** about 35 years in the wild and up to 50 years in captivity

# Glossary

**adaptation** body part or behaviour of a living thing that helps it survive in a particular habitat

**classify** group living things together by their similarities and differences

**conservation** protection or restoration of wildlife and the natural environment

**conserve** protect from harm or destruction

**elevation** height of the land above sea level

**endangered** living thing that is at risk of dying out

**evolve** change gradually over time

**extinct** living thing that has died out

**habitat** natural environment of a living thing

**mammal** animal that has fur or hair, gives birth to live young, and feeds its young on milk from the mother

**nutrient** substance that provides a living thing with the nourishment it needs to grow and live

**opposable thumb** thumb that can face and touch the fingers on the same hand

**rainforest** forest with tall, thickly-growing trees in an area with high rainfall

**species** group of similar living things that can mate with each other

**sub-tropical** regions of Earth that border the tropics

**tropical** regions of Earth around the equator

# Find out more

## Books

*Classifying Living Things: Classifying Mammals*, Andrew Solway (Raintree, 2009)

*Great Naturalists: Dian Fossey*, Heidi Moore (Heinemann Library, 2009)

*Looking for Miza: The True Story of the Mountain Gorilla Family Who Rescued One of Their Own*, Craig Hatkoff (Scholastic Press, 2008)

## Websites

**gorillafund.org**
Find out lots of information about gorillas and how people can help protect them on the website of the Dian Fossey Gorilla Fund International.

**www.bbc.co.uk/nature/life/Gorilla**
Learn about gorillas and other primates on this BBC website.

## Organizations to contact

**World Wildlife Fund UK**
**www.wwf.org.uk**
WWF works to protect animals and nature, and needs your help!
Have a look at their website and see what you can do.

**Endangered Species International**
**www.endangeredspeciesinternational.org/index.php**
This organization focuses on saving endangered animals around the world.

**Durrell Wildlife Conservation Trust**
**www.durrell.org**
This organization aims to help save animal species from extinction.

# Index